UNCOLLECTED

UNCOLLECTED

Uncollected: Poems of Love and Madness

MICHAEL ADELMAN

Library of Congress Control Number:		2019906264
ISBN:	Hardcover	978-1-7960-3181-2
	Softcover	978-1-7960-3180-5
	eBook	978-1-7960-3179-9

Print information available on the last page.

Rev. date: 06/05/2019

To order additional copies of this book, contact:
Xlibris
1-888-795-4274
www.Xlibris.com
Orders@Xlibris.com
796315

CONTENTS

SEA CHIEF WITH HANGING EYES

When I think of you
in November

madness and mischief
abound

I think of Sea Chief
with Hanging Eyes, a totem
in Victoria

whose servants
held on to his eyes
when he had to see,
when he had to cry,
when he was mad

as if medicine
were the tips of fingers
pressing against your eyes.

WINTER

kneeling
too cold to undress
her head at your feet

she wears a black sweater
beige pants, chunky shoes
her hair surprisingly
well coifed
to be thrust
on the floor

the black sweater pulls up
exposing the small of her back
in the dull light

a picture equals a 1000
        thoughts:

her skin is cold
your boots taste bitter
the room smells of leather
you hear pain

it's only a picture:
her skin cannot feel
her lips do not taste
nothing you smell or hear

DOMESTICITY

On Monday,
after the two barrels-
one with wheels, the other without-
are curbside, the rest is supplemental,
the orange peels, and wasted napkins
the miscellaneous bottles,
the bag of pasta my brother sent
last Christmas, the expiration date
mysteriously ripped off.

On Sunday,
which seems a lifetime before,
our intention was to beat the heat,
run early after a quick cup of coffee,
but we ended up otherwise,
my mouth on your vagina,
your lips on mine.
John came early
which meant microwave spaghetti
and lately I've come to shave him.

I always ask:
When did you last shave?
Oh, today, I just missed some spots.
A whole lot, I reply.
His beard is thick along the jawline
up under, close to the bottom lip
and hair grows – this is true –
on the corner of the lips themselves.
I wonder, is this unique to the mentally ill?

We're done and he wipes
the surplus shaving cream from his face.
Laundry washed and dried.
Sandwiches in the bag.
See you in a week or
See you in two, he's gone, and I am
left with running at noon.

The heat is unbearable.
At first I don't sweat and this is scary.

The sun burns my skin.
Beads of perspiration emerge.
Against my better judgment, I run.
I can only cool off by jumping
in the pool at the end of our street
where I join two mothers with
3 or 4 year olds in plastic wings
and a lawyer I know who married
a much younger lawyer who,
long legged and pretty,
shimmers in the heavy sun.

Later I go to the office,
happy on the ride in,
the Sox are winning despite a plague
of injuries, but when I leave
the truck won't start,
I call my son. He does not

reciprocate easily but agrees to drive
me home. I know I'll need another plan
for the morning. If we leave early,
the rest will unfold.

On Monday, by noon, the battery's
replaced. Later, when I arrive home
carrying the mail in one hand,
I return the barrels –
one with wheels, the other without.

FALLING LEAVES

My youngest son is mad.

Thanksgiving, I asked him to come early,
to clean the roof.
He was bleeding from the chin.

We considered, who would go up,
who would stay down, until
he divined the plot:
If he went up, I'd remove the ladder
and leave him there forever.
I climbed the ladder.

We fly through the air.
My son is the superman of madmen.
If he let's go, I fall.
If I let go, he sinks into oblivion.

My son is bleeding from the chin.
Blood mixing with leaves falling
to the ground, sinking into oblivion,
changing into the color of death,
and we ask: "Isn't it beautiful?"

I WOULD APOLOGIZE

1.

I would apologize if I could
I would traverse time to that dark night
when you said "no more."
I would apologize,
I would explain
the insult bore no fault

I would traverse time,
we would lie on the beach
tongue to tongue
victim to victim

I would proclaim innocence
and die at your feet.

2.

I would traverse time to that dark night
I would plead
and watch the snow descend.
I am innocent you proclaim.
"I did not know."

I would apologize,
I would explain
the insult bore no fault,
"I did not know."

3.

I would apologize if I could
I would traverse time to that dark night
I would feel the heat, touch the snow,
I would apologize if I could.

EDWARD HOPPER
(1882-1967)

in his self-portrait
hopper wears a wide-brimmed
hat his eyes appear blue
no rooms no windows
nothing to scare none of
the fearsome light
only his jacket is black.
a tiny bald man sits on a wooden sidewalk
he paints black
open windows
his light is too light
his light is the absence of black
a blonde in a blue dress leans
against the wall she wears black heels
you can't hear a word she says

MY MOTHER'S DISH

The night my mother
baked her head in our oven
(between 400 & 450° F.)
I led my brother
through ice and snowflaked dark
to House of Chin
where we ate Dinners for One
from plastic plates
designed to separate

rescued in Saybrook
from a dinghy gone awry,
the small boat tossed into the sea,
banned from Friday night movies,
I stick a needle in her foot.
I am the villain she loves to love,
from toxic birth to tic douloureux

cold, my father stands under the arc,
the tasty dish removed,
her body limp,
an empty bottle testament
to pain subdued by Scotch.

DROPPING THE TORAH

I am afraid of dropping the Torah,
Of the forty days and nights that follow,
Of a diet of bread and water.
I am afraid of the vortex of my dreams,
Uncontrolled, beckoning me to punishment.
Lashed to the pulpit,
I watch my mother, helpless, tearful,
Longing to feed me

Walking from the synagogue,
Friday night, holding hands, kissing,
The echo of a friend's nervous laughter,
Uncontrolled, shaming himself,
Before the congregation, were we to blame?
I am afraid of dropping the Torah,
Of the forty days and nights that follow,
Of a diet of bread and water.

At fifteen, while taking a leak in the bushes,
I lost God. So, you ask, thinking
I'm cornered like a cat's half-dead mouse,
What about dropping the Torah?
I smile. Forty days and nights,
A diet of bread and water,
My mother longing to feed me.

NOSTALGIA
For John

We eat pizza, our past
blinded by flourescent light.
We meet, talk of love,
our rendezvous caught
between past and present,
sandwiched between video rentals
and shopping lists.

You left, wandered
through rain forests and desert,
to return. We ache to touch.

MY MOTHER'S FUNERAL

My mother's name was Sally.
At her funeral,
the rabbi, new to town,
and friendlier to my father,
called her "Betty,"
and missed the broad meaning
of her life:
hidden candy, thirty years
of tic douloureux,
dismay and
an unsatiable need to manipulate.

We stand by her grave,
the December light is sharp,
each mourner shovels dirt
defining pockets of space,
her coffin left unsettled.

ALLIGATOR

Let me dress like you
Let me braid your hair
Let me tie your arms
and kiss your lips.

O' foul reptilian beast,
we were strangers then,
drawn to your cage
as flowers to a vase.

Let me kneel before your feet.
Let me understand the darkness.
Let me ride upon the waves
and drown beneath your tears.

O' cold and ancient beast,
my fingers twist the metal links,
your ghastly jaw and eyes
scowl in the noonday sun.

With slow ancestral bearing
we claw across the shallow
pool. The beast distills
and suffers loneliness.

THE TRIP

Seventeen miles from our house
to the group home,
the last five narrow and curvy,
turning

wilful at night,
with headlights
from a high-riding,
hard-bucking pick-up
malevolent and blinding,
bent on death and
destruction

yielding night and silence.

Can we mend the heart
with tiny fragments of love?

I DO NOT HAVE TIME

I do not have time
To let events seep
Like oolong tea,
Darken, find nuances,
Deeper meanings.
I do not have time.

Take the dinner party
Last Friday evening,
When the host uttered
Anti-Semitic remarks
About Jewing Them down.

Down where? I wonder.

The strange part is
That we stayed, did not
Create the proverbial scene
Or leave in a tizzy.

And the host and hostess,
Other than remarks that
Tore our hearts out,
Were kind and bid us
Farewell in the most
Heartfelt manner, standing

In their Doorway, smiling,
Canary pie was their last meal,
But I do not have time
To let this event seep
Like oolong tea,
Darken, find nuances
And the deeper meaning
Of their words, I do not
Have Time.

THE ART OF THE DOGON

We walk through the museum,
bemused by the art of the Dogon,

a man and woman of even stature,
carved out of ancient wood,

metal rings costume their faces,
each body reflecting the other

a quiver of arrows adorns his back
a child borne on hers.

we walk through the museum,
bemused by the art of the Dogon,
touched by their embrace.

TO BEN ADELMAN
1908-2005

Since your death
The seasons seem to pass more quickly.

In April, when you died,
The possibility of summer felt uncertain.

Today, the heat is unrelenting,
Only a chance of rain gives hope.

Although you died in April,
Your death felt autumnal

Flowers killed by frost,
Embers in a dying fire.

Ghosts plagued the last
Winter nights, the end of life

Was near and quiet.

THE HEEL OF THE FOOT

1.

I enter the room. Wait.
She enters. Orders me to kneel.
To kiss her feet.

My tongue luxuriates her toes,
Licks the crevices of her sole,
Finds the contour of her heel.

2.

A vision 30 to 40 years from now.
I am dead.
An old man whose feet flop,
More hobble than limp.

The old man is my son.
He was twenty-four, I recall,
Jumped the ledge, heels
Cracked like eggshells.

She orders me to crawl.
My eyes are transfixed
On the contours of her heel.

TAKEN

I loved you too much, too hard,
it made me afraid to speak,
to ask if we could be together
any night would do,
I knew the weekends were taken

Still, we kiss,
but that comes later
after long silence,
and then you leave.

Once, I saw you across the bay.
At least I like
to think it was you.

And once, in a dream
we were lovers. You
were caught, devoured,
and I forgot because
dreams, well dreams are like that.

Once, you came to my room,
and I spent more than I should
and we walked along a river,
you made your intentions clear

So, what should I do?

I look here and there
and remember you are gone,
a ghost, a filament to the past,
taken

Was it really you
across the bay?

RAPED

Raped, she felt him
pierce her eyes

She was bound,
if not, she'd touch his lips

She thought of yellow
daisies along the road

If his tongue lingered,
she would swallow him whole.

She thought of orange marigolds
and lilacs in the snow.

When he left,
she thought of peonies

and when he pierced her
eyes, she thought of tears.

ANALYST
To Joe Jacob

I can hear his patient laugh
and exit, although the suite
is designed not to embarrass.

We sit across
in hard back chairs
the couch is vacant, unused.

He is tall, white-haired,
Southern.

His long, slender fingers
punctuate the air with
phallic missives.

I think of him,
tremulous voice,
like ghosts, we travel
dark corridors,
sail empty seas
monsters lurk at every turn.

I wonder,
is he still alive.

BETRAYAL
For *Rilke*

An old woman looks back.
She irons, sews, prepares the next
Meal. He is standing
There, the same night many
Years before. Their bodies
Cold and wet, a late night swim.
They share a towel, kiss, dress
And run to meet his bus. That
Night is gone. She hears the rumor
Of a rumor. His family disapproves.
"They're much too young."
"You know, her father's just a butcher."
"We must act before it's too late."
"Enough," she says. She hurls
His ring upon the ground.
"I don't care what they say,"
He pleads. She turns and leaves.
She loathed, she hurt, she ached
With sorrow.
She looks him in the eye. Now,
Not to recant, but to elucidate.

And he is older too.
At first he missed her voice,
Longed to touch, watch her eyes,
Nothing,

Not the rumors, not the attitude
Were his. Betrayed,
Juliet would not be dead. He looks
Into a mirror and sees not
Deeds, not denial, but the
Monster she came to hate.
Like Orpheus he meant no harm
But, their words foretold her fate
His too.

DETROIT: NOVEMBER, 1969

Ron and I enter the Willis Bar
on a Sunday afternoon.
November is cold this year.
We drink cheap white wine.
Rituals of seduction and lust abound.

Nervously, Bonnie and I ascend
to our room, rented
by the hour, her black skin
luminescent amid the clutter
and disrepair. Our sex is hard
and unrevealing.

Later, Ron and I walk the streets,
Darkness camouflages their desuetude,
a cold wind hails against our faces.
Even now, a hint of fire in the air.

Two years before,
mayhem and madness descend.
A fierce disquiet erupts,
love and fear recoil.

GERONIMO

I thought Geronimo was cool
Not the plaster-faced cavalrymen
Not the John Waynes and William Holdens
But the Apache Indian, whose face was so lined
And body so sinewy that his shadows were one
With the mesas and the rocks and the dirt-dry landscape
Where the Cowboys and Indians roamed
In Hollywood's black and white imagination.

I saw *Fort Apache* in Boston, with Grandma Bea
In a movie theater where you entered on Tremont,
Walked through a tunnel and bought tickets a street away.
Later, I thought Cochise in *Broken Arrow* was cool
But not cool like Geronimo, and wondered why
Technicolor made Geronimo the bad guy.

Then, today on CNN, I heard Prescott Bush*
And other skullduggeries stole Geronimo's head
From a graveyard in Fort Sill, Oklahoma
Where Indian prisoners of war were buried.
His skull lies in a state of unrest, encased,
At Yale, in New Haven, in the State of Connecticut.

The newscaster spoke of a curse.
The Elis denied the skull was his.
No matter. After all these years, I still think
Geronimo is cool, cooler than Cochise.
And, despite the denials, I understand the curse.

* George H. W. Bush's Father; George W. Bush's Grandfather

THE POET'S NOW DEAD UNCLE

My uncle returned from World War II,
disembarked in Manhattan,
where women sold their wares
atop dimly-lit, narrow stairways.
He took the train home,
greeted by how great he looked.
A month later, he collapsed,
malarial fever and chills. Delirious,
he spent days in the extra bedroom
my mother (his sister) prepared
for my uncle's illness.

A scandal, something to do with a woman
he was not supposed to do something to,
resulted in a hasty trip to Florida
and his marriage three months later.
When we moved, my mother and father,
my brother and I,
the extra bedroom stayed behind.

My uncle worked, prospered,
lived in a lovely white house atop a hill.
When I was twelve, I cut his lawn.
My uncle was a whiz at bridge,
even better at poker, the money
was his for the taking.
Our paths diverged, and crossed only
at family weddings and other occasions.

In his sixties, my uncle took up golf,
a strange choice for a sedentary,
malarial man. He died at eighty
from heart disease, not a quick, sudden attack,
but a slow teasing death, the kind
that hints if you change your ways,
you can beat the odds. But, he didn't.

GIANT
for Amy

If I were a giant
I could touch the horizon
and catch your star,
hold the moon
between my hands,
hold back hot, molten lava,
and turn rivers into streams,
oceans into ponds.

But, I am not a giant.
your star fades over the horizon,
the moon belongs to the night,
lava kills, and
rivers run into the ocean,
and I? I lie beneath your feet
licking your soul with fire.

DECAYED MEMORY

The first place
was the second-story apartment
on Lincoln with the sun porch
and my uncle's extra bedroom
when his malaria relapsed,
and magic cement casements --
horses after a movie or tanks
to fight the Nazis,
and the cache in the back, buried
behind an old fence --
horse chestnuts, penny nails,
odd pieces of wood, candy and gum,
instruments of decayed memory.

PHOTOGRAPH

A black man talks
on the telephone. He
stands beside a liquor store.
He wears a suit, no tie,
a yellow turban, a large
cross dangles down his chest,
he smiles into the moon,
he sways to the music.

MY GRANDFATHER'S STORE

In my grandfather's store
open on Thursday night:
rows of empty beds
and unlit lamps,
an alcove of appliances.

A tall bald man
stooped behind a cage
bedazzles us with figures.

The elevator ascends
from dream floor
to dream floor,

and at the summit
another man, gaunt and thin
mends broken furniture
and keeps dark
secrets of the universe.

LOBLOLLY

In New Orleans
we view a loblolly pine
planted
from seeds taken to the moon,
as if seeds from the moon
were cleansed
and this tree shorn
of history.

COMING TO MISSISSIPPI

We left Detroit in a blizzard,
traveling South
Cincinnati, Louisville, Nashville,
Birmingham,
traveling
from point of view
to point of view.

After Louisville,
the sky cleared --
a hint of warmth.

We arrived at noon,
winter's barren fields masked
by loblolly pines and mid-day sun.
Damp and cold would follow.

THE BALLAD OF CARMEN AND MARIE

Night filled with strange images:
a man shot from his horse,
a lost dog wanders home,
Carmen and Marie watch from their room
in the drive-in movie theater,
watch dead mummies rise,
soldiers sing and soldiers die,
watch from their strange abode,
deep in the drive-in movie theater.

Exhausted, the last image fades,
Carmen and Marie sleep,
unlocked from their aural fantasy,
cars race to the exit,
dirt and dust fly,
the blank screen a ghostly apparition
haunts the deep night.

Like the final frame,
frozen against the dark October sky,
the drive-in movie theater closes,
Carmen stays, Marie leaves,
her strange movie abode
replaced by a self-service storage unit,
where she and her husband live
and sell hand-carved objects d'art:
beady-eyed birds of prey.

This is the ballad of Carmen and Marie.
They lived in a drive-in move theater.
One left, the other stayed.
Custodian of dust and decay.

WEIGHT WATCHERS

Flesh, straining against a soft prison,
a belt too tight,
the neck width expands,
but then slow shrinking escape
of waist and buttocks and thighs,
until the soft prison door unlocks.

I KNOW A MAN

I know a man
a gnarled, wizened man
I know a man
a tattooed, worthless man

I asked:
what do you do?
He replied:
"Gambler and petty thief."

I know a man,
a toothless, violent man
I know a man
a troubled, hopeless man

On a hot August day,
he was tried,
convicted,
sentenced.

I knew a man
a small, heartless man
I knew a man,
hanged, today at dawn

POETRY AND JAZZ

There is poetry in jazz
and poetry in the Lakeside Motel,
phone - television - carpet,
and jazz too,
and I imagine your white
buttocks deep in the crimson
carpet, and there is poetry in
the Sunshine Square Baptist Church,
Carson, Mississippi,
sharing space
with Sallie's Beauty Salon,
and at night, in the cold darkness
a distant voice beckons.
I strain against the static airways
to hear the music and the words.

WEST

We went West,
a quartet of young men,
marched into the desert
ate Basque food, in
a solitary restaurant,
burned by water and sand,
fought in Reno, and
differed on aesthetics.

We were lost
in California, searching
for Allen Ginsberg or Jack Kerouac,
but found thin, beady-eyed
girls who hung on bannisters
and drank tequila.

Alone, we yearn
to touch, but separate.
Our paths diverge
each step retreats
until the page is blank.

WILLIE SABU

Willie Sabu was a big white cat
with piercing blue eyes,
who appeared propitiously
in our yard one day,
having blazed a path
through woods and neighborhood,
leaving his scent
as if scent were a scepter
and we his dominion.

Willie's death was mysterious.
His big, sinuous body shrank.
His death concluded in a cardboard box
I carried to his last rightful owner.

From what source did this big white cat,
hungry for table food and bluejays,
draw power and definition?

VISITING DAY AT THE COUNTY JAIL

They wait,
huddled together
a patchwork quilt
of race and sex,
more black than white
older women
their heads propped
against the wall,
children who wander
in and from the pack
almost all are poor,
a young woman dressed in heels,
inviting speculation and desire,
Brueghel himself
would paint this scene;
the day's visitors caught
by electronic eye,
blind to the forces
that drive us to this place.

VERTIGO

Do you remember? I do.
We watched *Vertigo* at a drive-in --
really you watched the movie,
I sucked your neck.

I wanted to be your slave,
but didn't know how.

I wanted to kiss your feet,
suck the crevices between your toes,
but your carotid would have to do.

Remember? I was a secret between lovers.
After we parted, I watched you from across
a small bay. You were a lifeguard,
I was a lowly weekend busboy.

I slept in a room without doors,
ate rolls turned to stone,
dreamed of your long legs
and aquiline nose.

Do you remember Boston?
We made contact for the last time.
A dinner I couldn't afford,
your hasty farewell,
Did you have another lover stashed away?

Went to one morbid reunion,
maybe ... but I know better,
no listing in the alumni directory.
I scan the pages anyway.

If you're still alive and
read this poem, give me a call,
I'm in the book.

NOSTALGIA
For John

We eat pizza, our past
blinded by florescent light.
We meet, talk of love,
our rendezvous caught
between past and present,
sandwiched between video rentals
and shopping lists.

You left, wandered
through rain forests and desert,
to return, imprisoned
by the moon, betrayed
by memory and nostalgia

9-11-01

The night we danced
we rode the elevator into the sky.
A dancer from the Bronx,
tall and lean, reminded me
of Joe DiMaggio.

Ghosts tango across the room,
their heads bandaged and bloodied.
A hand reaches up from below,
overhead the skies darken,
the day is lost.

We look at paintings,
eat lobster, catch a matinee —
in the fall, leaves turn gold
and die. We waltz on powdered
snow, the sky is overcast.

Our carriage leaves at noon,
the horses buck, we swirl and dip,
our legs ride high. We dance across
the room. The metal twists,
the sky is void, the day is lost.

IF YOU'RE BLACK

If you're black and maybe twelve
And it's an unseasonably warm Saturday in December
And if it's you and your kid sister
She's, say, ten
And there is a fence
And you climb over or under
Or sneak through
And you both ride swings
And there's a cop
And a shot and you succumb

To which God do you pray?

TO M.C.

The first poem to you is lost.
Not to be found,
not on Word
nor Word Perfect
unsaved unstored undeleted.
Lost.

We were never lovers,
but I may have loved you.
I wanted you to see me
as james dean wearing a charcoal gray
sports jacket in *rebel without a cause.*

We were born in the same month
in the same year, but you longed
for someone older. You said,
"James Dean isn't real."

Under "C" in a our class year book,
you love shopping, theater and a certain
Mr. Right. I could have replied,
"Mr. Right isn't real."

News of your death came late.
If I remember, you died in California
not long after the birth of a child
and a kidney transplant. The
first poem had the sequence right.

SOLID OAK

The contract called for solid oak,
but when an arm rest came unglued,
we came face to face with truth. Particle
board hid beneath the wood, even worse,
beneath the cushions, deep blue to match
our carpeting, sheets of pine cracked,
filling the sanctuary with a sound so terrible
our reverend's sermon ceased to count.

Deacons met. "Our papers promised
solid oak."
"I'll takes pictures and write a letter,"
their lawyer said. "We're the third
oldest church in the state." "Afro-
American," old Ben Thompson added.

Things improve, times are good.
The pews gnaw. A garbage truck sidles
down an ally. Street lights turn amber at dusk.
The crime rate's down, the Mayor boasts,
"I'd like your vote." But, the benches crack,
The wood erupts, a tattered couch, bodies
sway among the pines.

"ROBERT YOUNG TRIES SUICIDE"
(Headline in <u>USA Today</u>)

Robert Young tried suicide,
but betrayed
by a dead battery,
he sits behind the wheel
the light is dim
the engine dead,
a fallow hose winds about his heart.

EYES

He cannot, cannot touch my eyes
his tongue swirls inside my soul
he takes my heart and mounts it like a horse
he says my eyes are like the winter sun
I say, kiss my lips, but he grabs my hair
a dagger pressed against my throat
I cannot, cannot betray my eyes
he cannot, cannot touch my eyes

TOUCH

I remember when we touched
our fingertips in a
pool of water
and I felt the shock.

I remember when you changed
shoes, and your foot
arched forward,
my tongue ached.

THE GREAT MASTURBATION FANTASY OF 1951

occurred in November
when the poet
encountered an advertisement
in the *The New York Herald Tribune,*
a woman of great style and beauty
her feet encased in black heels,
her legs cast a spell
and he came pinioned by
tears of ink, and
stained his mother's rug.

UNTITLED I

A plants'
blossoms
reach
oblivion

You reach up,
I am only a dream.

CHARLOTTE ON TIME

Charlotte on time.
Charlotte taxis to the gate.
Charlotte the puppet.
Charlotte the puppeteer.
Charlotte undresses.
Charlotte of wide hips and hawk-like nose.
Charlotte cries when she hears the news.
Charlotte on her death bed.
Charlotte on time.

SHE SAID SHE MIGHT

She said she might
but never would

She tied my hands
to touch my cock

I kissed her shoes
to taste her feet

I am clever by half
seduced them all:
tied my feet
gagged my mouth
felt their lash
swallowed their cum

she said she might
but I never could.

NORMAN

Sun
after rain,
my friend Norman
and I play with scraps of wood,
submerged in puddles,
skunk cabbage
permeates, my hands
tied behind my back,
I am
a villain easily captured,
sentenced to be tortured,
we march to a clear
stream a mile behind
his house.

boys will be
rapists, predators,
villains, addicts,
cheat on their income tax,
weak at foreplay,
cowards and cuckolds

before he moved, like
me, Norman lived in town,
on Lincoln Ave. His house
in East Great Plains was
miles away,
on a dust-laden road,
on the edge of a vacant moon.

boys will dream of crimes,
unbearable feats, whips,
a ship to sail, bondage,
revolution, and how life
dissolves with each new move.

SNAKES

One week-end
The women took the kids
To Dauphin Island.

Elliott and I drove up to Forest
To meet Nick and fish.
Nick is now dead.

We ate chicken fried steak
In a dimly lit cafe,
Learning *chicken fried*
Were the operative words.

And found Nick
Waiting on his porch
Fishing rods leaning
Against a post,
A rifle nestled in his lap.

"Snakes," he answered
When asked why the rifle.
As best I recall, Nick
Caught a bass or two,
Elliott and I nothing.
"The snakes must have
Jinxed us," I said, instead
Of good-bye or thanks

Nick died of a stroke
A year or two later
He was thirty-eight.
The day we fished,
Elliott and I drove home,
And I remembered the feel
Of the hot sun,
And our shoes wet
From the damp weeds and grasses
And how it would have felt
If Nick had really killed a snake.

DODGE-EM

Whack, bang, bam!
terrified even
in my father's arms
fearful, loathsome bumper
cars chalky headlights
frames outlined by strips
of rubber grilles like
Halloween masks
electricity crackling
from ceiling down poles
driving towards each
collision, want to ride
the dodge-em, I'll hold
you. You.

96 years old,
calls during the week
confused about where
he is or when we go
coaxed into dressing
for breakfast, fears
not death but dementia
when did I become unafraid

DREAM GIRL

I.

her long legs roam
the room is gray and dark
a foot is missing
cracked fragments
of a tiny kiss we
touch we can't
leave she weaves
her art she has no arms
is this a dream

II.

my hands bleed
tied to the steel frame
she washes the blood
my feet are cuffed
the thick leather cuts into skin
she clamps my tongue and weaves
a chain into my heart

III.

the room is cluttered
toes for me to suck
violent eyes
a pair of lips
spikes hammered
into my hands and feet

IV.

the shadows begin to dance
the room is silent
we rise together
our limbs turn from
heel to head *Mein*
Herze schwimmt im Blut
she sings we rise together
our lips touch